The Feelings of Life with All It's UPS & DOWNS

Redbonetrouble Life as I Know It to Be

VOLUME NO. 1

Terralisa McBride

authorHOUSE®

AuthorHouse™
1663 Liberty Drive
Bloomington, IN 47403
www.authorhouse.com
Phone: 1 (800) 839-8640

Published by AuthorHouse   06/11/2015

ISBN: 978-1-5049-1673-8 (sc)
ISBN: 978-1-5049-1672-1 (e)

Library of Congress Control Number: 2015909146

Print information available on the last page.

Full Biography:

Born 4-19-1971 in Flint, MI to Linda Gist & James Williamson (both deceased now). I have two siblings that share the same mother as I and I have four siblings that share the same father as I. As I grew up poverty was a way of life not an image, There were things I've seen that most young children should have never been a witness too. Early in my teenage years I found the love of words. I began to explore my writings with simple notes to inspire family and close friends. When I became a mother I felt a new wave of refreshing energy fill up within, it was almost like being flushed with water throughout my entire body. All my emotions were pure and clear to me.

It was at that time I knew my thoughts and feelings of my surroundings had become one with me. As I approached different people or was involved with different events my soul latched on to the aura that filled the air. Then one day it was all just a blur. I got involved with other activities that lead me astray from my true calling. However, I've always jotted down little passages and thoughts that moved me. It wasn't until my late 30's I decided to recapture my own inner self and search my soul to see if indeed this was meant to be.

Now that my life is on a new path. I vowed to make a lifelong passion become as real as I am as I stand here on this earth.

Terralisa McBride

POEM TITLES FOR MY
FIRST POETRY BOOK
THE FEELINGS OF LIFE WITH
ALL IT'S UPS & DOWNS

MIND:

Sometimes I feel I'm losing my mind, sometimes I sit alone in the dark and just cry. There are a lot of things bottle up inside of me I can't explain, but all in all I'm still the same. I am the only one who understands me and knows my pain; I am the only one who seems to carry the blame. Deep down inside I am so alone, I'm always sitting listening for the phone, although when it rings there is never a comforting voice on the other end (I still pick it up) It's always a person who's problems are greater or equal to mine and that person feels that he/she is losing their mind.

WHEN YOU ARE ALONE:

When you are alone your mind begins to wonder, your thoughts and feelings come to reality while your soul feels like the sound of thunder. When you are alone your mind is at peace, when you are alone your problems in the world are ceased. When I am alone I express my feelings on paper. When I am alone my mind feels safer. I think of each and every way possible to better myself and when I tell someone it seems that they just put it on the shelf; A shelf that is used to store many thoughts, a shelf that is used to store many faults. Could this be the reason why people like to be alone?

IN ANY EVENT:

In any event there is a beginning and there is an end. But for any event there is also a sin, a sin in which only the person in question can defend. In any event your self-esteem is judged; In any event your heart needs to be unplugged. Relieved of all your hurt and shame, relieved of all the bitterness and confusion that makes you insane. In any event at the end you are the blame even if at the beginning you thought you were sane. So take heed to these events and mellow out your life fast, because in any event it could be your last!

THE DARK SIDE:

It's dark, cold, wet & dreary, so alone you get weary. The dark side creeps up on you like a stolen moment with power. It haunts your soul each and every hour. You beg for the day you scream for some light. The dark side has taken over; you fight with all your might. The dark side is that grey area you find within your soul. When you're all alone your mind wonders & takes control.

MILES AWAY:

When someone you love is miles away, you wonder about them every day. You wonder how their life is changing in each and every way. The road between you seems forever but just remember and never say never, because you can hug this winding road with your mind and put the miles between you behind. Your soul fits the road like a hand in a glove - because there is a greater love. And even though your body is miles away your spirt lives within me with each passing day.

It was the summer of 1986; other teenagers were making plans for a fun filled summer vacation. I was just glad that school was finally out, and no more homework needed to be done at home. At that moment I had seen the strangest thing occur. This guy was on the back of a garbage truck doing what seemed to be his normal thing.... then BAM!!!! A car slams into the back of the garbage truck and the guy on the back screamed out so loud that I felt his pain.

The car had completely severed his foot from his leg, and the shoe he was wearing was in the street with the foot still in it. OUCH!!! The look on his face was as if he just seen his life flash in front of him. As one on looker got out of their car to check on the driver of the car, the man who just lost his foot crawled to retrieve his body part and began to untie the shoe and pull the foot out. At that moment he passed out and the ambulance had arrived just in the nick of time.

INSIDE OF ME:

Imagine the darkness, imagine the cold & heat, imagine the sharpness remember the agony of defeat. How about strength & weakness, how about sharp & sweetness, how about tainted ways and lonely days, maybe brightness may be sun, maybe life has just begun. In & out without a doubt, in & out will make you shout, Curse & Scream - inside of me is just what it seems.

EMPTY THOUGHTS:

A picture say's a thousand words that you could never hear, a picture with empty thoughts could show many things that are not very clear. Beautiful settings, amusing shots a picture could fill your head with several thoughts. A picture holds a place in time with memories your mind can rewind. There are pictures you could stare at for days & there are pictures you quickly put away. You have pictures buried deep in your mind you tend to hide; but brought out by a jester or fault --- hmmmmmm - A Picture with empty thoughts.

WHY/ANSWER/QUESTIONS/TRUTH/LIE:

Now those are power words that can make you or break you. Besides, WHY ANSWER a QUESTION with a LIE when the TRUTH always stands out.

FRIEND:

Hello friend what's going on, has life been playing that same ole song? Don't give in just be strong & remember that sometimes things do go wrong. By being yourself and staying ahead you'll always be able to make the bread. A friend indeed is also a friend in need. I'll be your friend even when you bleed. Although some skies are grey and others are misty blue, I'll be your friend even when we're 92. Sometimes problems occur when you're not ready; I'll hold your hand and keep you steady. I won't say good bye when you're gone away. I'll just remember all the better days.

IN FACT IT'S ALL A LIE:

Am I kidding myself when I say I love you? Am I forcing myself to believe it's true? If so I wonder why or in fact is it all a lie. You promised to be there for me under any circumstance, I promised to give you another chance. Who's playing mind games, who's willing to give it a try when in fact it's all a lie. Is this what life is about or is this how it ends? Some people die some survive maybe in fact it's all a lie.

WHO AM I?

When the weather breaks and the ice is no more, you tend to look for me out your back door. Sometimes I'm round, Sometimes I'm Square; however, my smell will fill the air. When you want to relax & chill fill me up & you will. Check out my frame & fill it full of meat, on a nice day this is something you can't beat.

Will you sit, watch me & glare while my sparks shoot fire in the air? I'm hot can't you see, I burn like hell to the third degree. But this is a burn you will yearn, hold your horses & wait your turn. I'm good for plenty of more uses, once your meat hits the heat there will be lots of juices. If you like what you hear read between the lines and sigh... It will make you wonder WHO AM I?

(Grill)

I HAVE MANY NAMES:

There are a lot of things you remember from each journey you pass, a lot of those things you hold dear and want to last. I chose names because that is my common ground names people tend to remember with each whispering sound. The name I was given starts with a letter "T" this initial throws me through three's. Terrifying Trouble, Tremendous Turnovers, Taunting Tactics, it makes you wonder why I like this. I have many names and I love them all from Mom to Monster, from Terrible-Lisa to RedBone Trouble these are names my mind seems to cuddle.

MY MAN:

One last tear I shed for you will be the first step I take finding a new. A man to take care of me, my boy, and my girl, a man who would change my whole damn world. A man who can deal with a relationships ups and downs, a man who would show me around the town. Dealing with my ways of life than that's the man who I'll become his wife. A man I'll bleed for a man I adore, a man who will put my past behind and close the door. The man I need and who can see the things that I can see, then that will be the man meant for me --- MY MAN.

Fall 1987 I was 16 and just about ready to deliver my first child. I had been through a lot, because my mother & father were alcoholics so I had to take on the roll as both parents and care for my younger brothers. Now that was not an everyday walk in the park, I mean it was like I had 4 children and one on the way. Sometimes I had to just sit and force a smile on my face to hide the shame and the pain. My brothers and I had to share so many things; like clothes, toys, and even food.

As I pondered how my life would turn out to be, I never forgot the things I had to endure that actually got me to this point. Seriously, I felt like the weight of the world was resting on my shoulders and the life growing in my belly would have to live life filled with violence & drugs. Hell, I was just a child myself; I never knew that I'd lose my mom before I was a woman.

IF YOU WERE HERE L.J.G

If you were here Linda Jean Gist I wonder what would you say, about all the changes my life goes through each and every way. Would you back me up, or step aside? Would you hold my hand and be my guide? When I

5

make a mistake would you criticize me and beat me till I'm blue? Or would you hold my hand and help me start a new? When I lost you I lost my best friend, When I lost you my life seemed to end. If you were here my life wouldn't be so bad, if you were here my life wouldn't be so sad. Today is your birthday you would have been another year older but the calm winds swept you away, when I need to cry I don't have your shoulder.

CHILDREN

Children these days are coming up fast, Children of yesterday are a thing of the past. Children today are considered as young adults, young adults today are considered last, while grandparents are a thing of the past. Who claims responsibility for the children? Who cares if the run wild? This could even mean your child. If we were animals and brought up in the wilderness we would know the meaning of children-less, because out in the wild you're no longer a child.

MOTHERS DAY

Mother's Day is a special day you celebrate once a year, but Mother's Day is everyday let's get this clear. Mother represents something strong & bold, treat your Mother with respect is what you're told. Every day you wake & breathe honor thy Mother if you know what I mean. With respect, with pride, your mother is your inside. Mother's Day not just today or tomorrow But Mother's Day is everyday so be sincere, Mother's Day is everyday let's get this clear.......

THE LITTLE GIRL IN THE SHELL

Open up let me out; please... please... don't make me shout. Its dark in here I cannot see, the air is thin I can hardly breathe. I have been in here far too long I've forgotten my favorite song. If anyone is out there that can hear my cry; this is not a bluff I am a beautiful girl; A Diamond in the Rough. A lonely woman who feels like a little girl, hidden away from the world. Why was I chose to be kept in a shell surely it was not for protection because this feels like hell. I want to be free to grow and become a woman, I want to see what it feels like to become a woman, and I want to feel the touch of a man like a woman. The little girl in the shell lives there no more, The young lady who you were afraid to let glow, is truly a woman you don't know.

DO YOU REMEMBER?

Do you remember being a child?
Do you remember running wild?
Do you remember all the times you got into trouble?
Do you remember when your parents were at your side on the double?
Do you remember when you didn't have to worry about a thing?
Do you remember the sound of your allowance Cha-Ching?
Do you remember making a good grade?
Do you remember all the toys you had to trade?
Do you remember anything as a child?
Well you're all grown up now why are you still running wild?

My daughter learned to crawl in the spring of 1988, her father was much older than me so he did not see her much during that time. I guess my family thought that he would not be around much anyway to help raise her. However, he did seem to want to be in her life more than they knew. He was well known in the streets, and most people were afraid of him. The people he hung around all had bad reputations and did all kinds of things like stealing cars, breaking into the homes of hard working people and even strong arm robbery. I knew this was not the kind of person I'd want to be associated with, but the image of having a hardcore B-Boy around did seem pretty cool, at least to a young girl.

However, a lot changed when he first laid his hand on me in a way my own father has never did. The love I thought I had for this man had now become fear. There were times I did not know if he was going to really hurt me bad or just keep that fear in my heart as a tool he could use. This type of mental & physical abuse continued for the next year and a half. When I made my mind up to get away from him, I did; I took my daughter and left in the middle of the night. This was a strong powerful moment for me. Really, it was the first time I felt like a woman, a mother protecting her child. But once again several months later he caught up with me; and as I picked myself up off the ground making sure there was no glass piercing through me from the glass dinette table he just slammed me on. I still felt like a strong woman with pride, I was not going to give up or give in I fought back and I made sure he knew that was the last time. By the winter of 1989 I had finally graduated from an adult high school, I had my own home and a part-time job. I found it very relaxing when I was doodling on paper with words and images that constantly ran through my mind. I truly believe that was the moment I felt writing was good for my soul.

WHY I WRITE

Why I write is a simple reason, why I write throughout the season, because it's a way of expressing myself, and it's a way of relieving myself, from all the criticism, hurt, pain and blame. Because these are truly the things that gets done to me the most. They say the pen is mightier than the sword; I believe its right, because neither the pen nor the paper has put up a fight. It's harder for me to say words than it is to write words. Maybe it's better said that my mind works better than my mouth. Everything I read I recite, maybe that's the reason I write.

TO START A NEW!!!

Nervous, Scary, Calm, Excited, Wondering if you're welcomed or invited. Smile, Laugh, Seek to understand, Choose to win & Try to fit in. To start something new is an experience you must overcome; to start something new is a wonderful feeling, like life has just begun. There is a first time for everything which will soon be a thing of the past; however, first impressions do last. Keep going strong you won't go wrong, so own this new start and own it in your heart.

YOU HAVE THE RIGHT

As the years passed by people either grow together or grow apart, sometimes they lose site on what's right or what's wrong. You have the right to respect your life and be prosperous to grow; you do not have the right to issue a dirty low blow. You have the right to be happy, beautiful, loving & kind, you don't have the right to disrespect people and keep them behind.

Holding one back from their own beliefs is a selfish tactic, that you choose not to see. You have the right to make your own decisions in life even if you are a husband or a wife. You do not have the right to force someone in to love or fear especially to someone near and dear. You have the right to get far away from the one that causes you agony and pain; you do not have the right to make a person feel insane.

HUNGRY FOR LOVE

In the kitchen where everyone eats, certain stimulations arise from the heat. While bread is baking in the oven a husband & wife sneaks in some loving. We understand that your life with your man can be so sweet; I know you can stand the heat so bring on the goodies and treats.

Being a new mother tends to bring all kinds of attention your way. I mean, most guys already know you are having sex because you have a child and your body has taken on a women's form. It really doesn't even matter how young you look or how young you are, having a baby gives off all kinds of messages. I have never had the feeling of being a loose woman, even though my virginity was taken or shall I say given up at the tender age of 14. I soon found out that having a baby at 16 and hanging out with my friends gave off the wrong message to the wrong kind of people.

Most young ladies want to be married before they turn thirty, at least that's what I was told. It just seemed like most thirty year old women I knew had not too many good things to say about that message society has made us all to believe. I could not even imagine being married; I have always been to head strong to be tamed by any man. And knowing what I put up with from my daughters father Oh NO!! I would rather be alone.

IN TO YOU

There is a warm place in my mind that I can only visit for a few; this place allows me to be in to you! This fictitious trip in my mind is one of a kind that I truly indeed love to rewind.

As my day comes to an end I get so cold & blue, because my warm thoughts are in to you. My inspiration starts with each morning's dew, Oh-Me, Oh-My I can hardly wait to see you.

In to you with spirt, in to you with my mind, in to you with secrets I'm willing to hide. I'm in to you like water in oil; I'm so in to you my body boils.

FIRE & ICE

The combination of fire & ice, is nice twice because together it's warm. Such as the feeling of two people combined as one, which makes their love swarm. It's been told that hot & cold could never be mixed but when you re-kindle love that combination is fixed.

When one is cold as ice and the other is hot as fire something about it brings out desire. If you can deal with the heat and maintain the cold, you could warm your heart deep into your soul. Fire and Ice just say it twice this is a memory you can hold.

WAVES IN THE WIND

Strolling down the street feeling the rough pavement on the bottom of my feet. A cool breeze blows by,,, While my eyes are looking toward the sky,,, Howwww lovely does it feel oooh my-my-my-- waves in the wind crossing the sky, makes you dream of heaven way up high. High above the clouds,,, way past the blue,,, your mind is soaring the unknown not believing that it's true. Waves in the wind, Waves in the wind, Waves in the wind for eternity it flew...

PEEP

You become what you see avoid the lock and key get a little bubbly go with the flow. Look at the signs don't you know? Are you tipsy or wasted? Is your mind a little bogged? Can you hear what I'm saying or can you see past the fog? I want some Kool-Aid along with a "samich" hour after hour I'm ready to do some damage.

Although, I knew I wasn't ready to be married I did want to feel loved by a man. At this point in my life I had seen what it does to women who have not been able to experience a man's love; it really does something to the mind. It's funny how life throws you curve balls and sends you sliding into third base so fast that your head spins. My mother had passed away; my dad was not really in tuned with what my life was like with a baby girl, being a young girl myself. Besides he was on his own high, drug of choice at that time; crack cocaine.

My two younger brothers were just about tired of that way of life. And seeing that I had my own home (renting of course) they eventually came to stay with me and now I was just where I started before. Taking care of my brothers as if they were my own children, including washing clothes by hand, preparing meals, making sure they went to school and stayed out the streets. I will say this; my grandmother has been like a solid rock in my life. The struggle would have been that much harder if she was not here to help when I needed that loving, caring hand of a mother. This little woman (standing about 4'8") was the toughest women I'd ever met. She gave birth to nine children and still managed to keep a job, keep a roof over their head and feed them all. My grandfather was a hardworking man as well and together they made a life that I never knew would be a stepping stone building block for the foundation that my own life would follow. The look on my grandmother's face however, at the time my grandfather and mother had passed away, has been that same face of strength I would endure in times to come. Then I'd see my grandfather and my mother often in my dreams, and it made me recall my early child hood years.

I HEARD HIM SAY

I heard him say life goes on, I heard him say "My family and friends be strong". I heard him say don't you sigh, this is not the end so don't say goodbye. I heard him say life itself winds around a never ending track. You see it's like a haircut & shave it will come back. I heard him say when the light becomes dark and everything seems a little grey, I will surely see you again one day.

QUESTIONS

There are many questions that are unanswered and so many that are misled, why? There are many answers to questions that are wrong and there are many answers to questions that get prolonged, why? You cannot survive without questions and you cannot live without answers, why? To many questions, not enough answers, why? Sometimes when you ask too many questions you are called a fool, Sometimes when you have too many answers you are considered a know it all, why? Why is the world filled with so many questions or answers and not enough love, Why?

OPPORTUNITY'S & SMILES

When I think of exceeding and moving ahead, I'm very thankful for getting out of bed. You see; to excel in style is worth a smile because you know to reach any goal within a mile, an opportunity comes with a smile. When I think of ways to say I appreciate myself for who I am and what I have become, I often smile. Because a lot of mishaps can cross your path which will enable your ability for any opportunity and that alone can cramp your style. Smiles & Opportunities are all we have, so keep focus and on track because some opportunity's don't come back. A smile will last a mile just keep in mind that to rise above any situation, be the best you can be. No matter what city or town give it your all don't let negative vibes keep you from having opportunities and smiles.

MY KING

I woke up wanting you, I don't wear your ring but in my heart; you are MY KING. The age gap between us doesn't mean a thing; my destiny says you are MY KING. I don't know you, but I feel you. My heart is in your hand, you are a king, my kind of man. The Thought of you soaring through my mind generates moments lost in a memory that a message can barely describe. I would love to share this image with you as a worrier who informs his king. Just knowing you exist makes my heart sing because I now know that fate has carried me and brought me to MY KING.

COLORS OF LIFE

If I had a green dollar for every time I thought of you I could be filthy rich. If I spent all my time ignoring you with a black cold heart you would call me a bitch. Life is like a box of crayons (with many assorted colors), some you can mix & match while some don't blend well with others. I choose your color because you're my style with the right wrappings, length, and strength pound for pound. If you know your history, you would see that people like me and you were meant to be. Society might not like it turn and stare, But people like us are an unbeatable pair. There are two kinds of people that the media cannot touch, although when we are together it creates such a fuss. Colors, things we see in everyday life, some dull, some neon, or super bright. We are all colors in an assorted colorful world with all sorts of meanings. Don't be afraid to show your true colors in life you would be surprised to see how well you mix with others.

Thinking back as life seemed to be changing for me or shall I say growing on me. I started to write more. However, I found my words were more mature than I was and most adolescents my age. I had always wanted to be heard and loved it seemed that my words also had more experience than I had. Maybe it was because I have heard all kinds of quotes of life. I remember one time when I was 7 years old my mom said "red, don't you ever let anyone speak for you, always stand true to your own words how you want them to be heard". I lived by those words of wisdom my mom said from that moment. My upbringing was a little different than most. At least that's what I had grown to believe.

When things were low around the house, my grandmother always knew how to make ends meet. She would stretch stuff so much we would have left overs for breakfast the next morning. Each one of my cousins experienced life at "Grandma's house" which became a family tradition itself, every time we had the chance to reminisce about being young that was the most giving phrase. She is now in her late 80's and walking side by side with youth (smile).

I still to this day find it amazing that I still have her in my life. I love that the heavens above is allowing me and my family to enjoy her presence at this time in our lives. When I recall the day back in July 1987, the moment she walked into the front door returning home from work; it was just before 9:00 am. "Buddy,... Buddy,... chile is the man dead" My eyes got really wide, because you see I had been sitting and talking to him (with no response) all morning and not one second did I think there was a problem. I mean he was a very heavy snoring man but that morning I had not realized he had not made a sound.

As my grandmother instructed me (8 months pregnant) go get your uncle Lee upstairs; I moved swiftly. As Uncle Lee approached him and took one look at my grandfather he was like "oh yeah he's gone". I couldn't believe it; I was just having a conversation with him. When Uncle Lee lifted him up I seen the most horrific thing in real life, rigor mortis had sat in. I thought someone had beaten him in the back with a board. It was dark purple and red and looked kind of dry and flakey, hope I never have to see that again (is what I said to myself). I was 8 months pregnant when he died and my daughter was 9 months old when my mother died, how ironic.

But being a young mother still learning to be a woman was turning out to be one task I had not truly thought thoroughly. I was totally on a road to destruction if I did not continue to follow my path in life. But as any normal young you can't tell me nothing little lady in charge attitude took over; life took another twist for me.

EMOTIONAL STORM

A gentle thought comes to mind when I think of you. A warm soothing feeling I cannot explain, my body sweats like rain. The moisture overwhelms me inside and out, my thoughts, my mind, and my body screams without a doubt. Touch me won't you please, before I boil over, give me what I need. With your broad loving shoulders like wrought iron or brick boulders, the thunderous noise we make as the bed shakes all while we endure our perfect storm. This is my own forecast station can't you see, my emotions are the weather channel when you are near me.

SUMMER SUN

Can you hear the ocean's voice whispering in the air? I can see that it's speaking to me while I'm sitting in this chair. It wants me to be refreshed, cheerful & mellow it's calling out my name --- well, well, "hello". Sitting at the ocean the summer sun never seems to end, even when the sun sets your body wants to jump in. As the wiltering night begins to fall the ocean's voice seems very calm. Your presperating body has been influenced and heavily endured; the ocean has won again and led you to shore. As the stars began to light up the sky, you look at your chair and say good bye. The mind has taken over and your body must follow, to be refreshed before the hot summer sun tomorrow.

SWEET

Sweet is a word you say without taste, Sweet is a word you use when looking at a women's waist. As tender as it sounds you can't wait for the moment it's going down. You're excited and you have high hopes; your legs are trembling, the sweet smell is on your mind and know your backs against the ropes.

ME

When I look in the mirror oh my what do I see; a short body light brown and kind of round; a woman who looks like me. I love the skin I'm in, deep within my soul, heart of gold no one man can control. When I move about I move with ease and grace, I keep a pretty little smile on my face. No one can walk in my shoes, no one knows my pain. My life is as complicated as my name. I am trying to be me I don't want to be you. My favorite color is red not blue. My thoughts motivate me what about you? I am very happy with the joy I bring in my life no regrets only sacrifice; ME.

TODAY

I cannot get you out of my head because I'm always trying to get you in to my bed. When I close my eyes I see you, when I open my legs I feel you. When I hear your voice I melt, When I think of you I smile. When I am near you I forget where I am and when I am away I want to be where you are. This is my mental emotional thoughts of you today and pretty much every day.

Terralisa McBride

YOU

When I met you.... I found me.... although at this moment I know we could never be. The joy my heart feels sets my soul free. As my journey begins to unfold from thoughts of being a wife, my destiny caresses my mind. Because I no longer have to sacrifice.... My intentions.... my ways..... my long nights and days.... Free as a bird yet gentle as a lamb, the smile on my face reflects the person I am. Because of you I have found me, Because of you my life has reason to be.... Thank you!

It's really amazing how in life you encounter several different people and your mind opens up and now you have managed to make a new friend or enemy. I have noticed that life is so complex that no matter how much you attempt to do right, wrong issues still come about. At one point in life I almost gave up on the thought of putting my words on paper and making a change in my life. I watched a lot of family members go through some tuff times, and struggled with two or more children.

I was so nervous that my life would just be worthless because no one in my family had a good job, nor money set aside for whatever life put in their path. But we did have much love for one another, and I still feel that love is just as rich as having currency in the bank or in hand. One major thing I was taught is that family is everything. Never loose site on that, the people you love and live with are the ones you deal with.

CHANGE

Speaking to be heard, yet listening to think, sooths your thoughts until you blink. Memories and issues of days ago, long nights no sleep is no way to go. I heard someone speak about their thoughts with an open heart while others listened and played the part. Inner beauty shows deep within, lets a lovely soul shining through as we all know, a simple wind can shift life into a wicked storm, hold on peaceful nights will come by the morn.

TRUE BEAUTY

Love is a flower drenched by the rain. It can weather the storm and still blossom again.

STRENGTH

This Moment, This Day, This Time I plan to get it right. There was This One Time, On This One Day, I Thought of This One Moment I planned to get it right. Now About This Day, and About This Time, About This moment..... My plan to get it right has begun.

SEX

Tricks & Treats go hand in hand swisher sweets are a named brand. Piping Hot, Juicy wet, Steamed up mirror.... oh don't forget. Relaxing moments for stressful times, gives you a chance to unwind. Do not fight the feeling just let it roar, face reality don't close the door. Tasty thoughts fulfilling needs I'm not one to beg.... But please baby please.

WOMEN ON FIRE

Tantalize you, Tame you with pleasurer and tease you with desire. I'll give you all you need I am your women on fire. I am rich with love and respect; You bleed I bleed we both write checks. Fall to my knees worship you like a King, cater to your every move with nothing to prove. These are the many things I'll do for you, we got this, we own this, it is our empire. If the feeling is mutual, then I am your women on fire.

INNER THOUGHTS

Happy is a word, Soul equals me, Life is the result, now my heart is free.

Terralisa McBride

PEOPLE

We see lots of different people throughout our life time. It is kind of hard to keep in mind that the people we see are different; when you really see how they are. Sometimes you don't know a person until you see that person in their true form as he or she really lives life. It is like looking through a magnifying glass; it is there just not visible to the naked eye. People mask lots of things about their life, yet when the mask is off the person you see is not the person you have come to know. People are different throughout our life time, what you see is truly not what you get and that you need to know.

Growing up without a mother was not very easy. Sometimes I would find myself wondering if I would make it in this world long enough to see my own grandchildren. My daughter has never seen my mother, nor heard her voice. However, a very dear friend of mine did get a chance to meet my mother. Strangely enough it was a spiritual meeting. You see, my mother had been dead for 16 months and she spoke through my friend. I had a weird tingly feeling the moment my friend spoke to me. The message she brought to me was something my mother only said to me. "Girl never give up, the women you stride to be, is all in me. You become the lady that stands strong because the girl in you wants the woman to be strong". My entire body shook and trembled from some wave of refreshing coolness. I knew my mom was present at that moment.

THERE IS

What makes you believe that this is all your worth, what makes you believe you're on his turf. Screaming, Shouting, Fussing, & Cussing you out is this the best you could do.....I doubt. This is your life and your time, what happened to your mind? Girl Friend!!! Read Between the lines. There is hope, where is your pride, When will you get off this bumpy ride? I know how you feel and I'm just keeping it real. There is another out there, There is another who would care, There is another that will make you feel like no other and treat you like a queen and not like a little brother.

DONE

I'm ready to tell you it's time for me to go, I'm ready to tell you our love is no more. I'm sure this is not what you want or what you seek -- silence fills the air when I try to speak. Do you even care or are you aware what I want to tell you may not be fair. Things are not what they used to be. I'm not that same young girl you're not that same ole guy. Why must you think we should continue to try? I'm done it's over we are through, you have to understand you're not my boo.

THE THICKNESS OF YOU

When you hold me, When I hold you, The feeling I get is so true. Damn I love the thickness of you. At night or in the morning my mind is yearning, the throbbing, the heat, the agony of defeat; the sound of thrusting is such a treat. Oh my I want to creep, oh damn that's sweet the thickness of you has got me twisted and off my feet. The thickness of you has got me gone the thickness of you; Damn I want to Bone.

SIGNS OF A LEADER

Walk with your head up high, smile through the pain, laugh at your sorrows and never be ashamed. The gift we all endure is one in the same; we come from the earth while heavens bells rang. Stand strong never start a fight but be ready to give it your all if a match is in sight. You are a Queen or a King does loving yourself make you mean? Your heart is your gifted weapon it makes you feel beneath any situation. The brain has magical powers that give you thoughtful sight; it works really hard even while you sleep at night. The soul has life that gives you swagger it's the beauty that showers the world and makes you unique and that's all that matters. The sign of a leader is already with in you, just follow the signs and lead yourself into your destiny as the Queen or King were created to be.

NEVER BREAK

A steady drip of water can cause lots of damages to any substance in any form. It just beats the surface continuously ever more. When you want something bad enough you need to be like a steady drip of water. Never Break stride Never Break down, Never Break, Never Break your in control now.

HIM

Who are you? Where did you come from? I did not intend to meet you at a whim, that man, who? Him? I have passed him by before, down hallways and through doors. I didn't know him at all just seen him a few times. I believed it was time to meet him and see if he was meant to be mine.

At 18 I thought I was grown and living life to the fullest. I was my own women; I had a 2 year old child and my own home. One thing was missing however; this was something I had never truly believed I would do. But it happened, I had ran into a guy (whom I had met previously in high school) while shopping at the local meat market. We did not exchange numbers but we shared a few friendly smiles and a very short conversation. Shortly after that we hooked up and BAM!!! I was expecting another child and then he moved in with me. All though I had been through one hell of an ordeal with this man, I continued to stick with him for what it was worth. I truly wanted a family and to be someone's wife, I just was not ready for that life.

I was 21 years old by the time I gave birth to my son, I had come up with several names but when I was unconscious from the Cesarean (C-Section) I just had on this cold 13th day of February, his dad decided to name him after him with the roman numeral II after his name. When I came home from the hospital, I was beginning to really feel like a mom, my daughter was very bright and well spoken. My new baby made me re-think my life once again as a young un-wed mother with 2 kids with 2 different daddies. I had a lot of growing up and thinking to do if I was going to be the best at this motherhood thing. I had no regrets however, I did wonder what if?

A LIFE OF LOVE

Living life to the fullest is the greatest love of all loving the one you're with throughout that time is worth it all. A life of love brings you so much joy, A life of love is like a brand new toy. Life and love are two individual dreams come true love and life is something meant for two. I'm so happy to have found a life of joy and love with you. When we married I felt my life expand, and my love for you grew. I could never imagine life or love without you!

THE LIFE THAT I LIVE

The life that I live is a complicated one; the life that I live is sometimes fun. My life gets changed as the days come, my life its self is a weary one. Sometimes in my mind I wish I would die, but the more I think it I know it's a lie. There are two reasons that are keeping me alive, and those two reasons have gleaming eyes. Eyes that see me threw my worst times, and also see me as the days go by. The life that I live is a ridiculous one; the life that I live is a critical one. The life that I live will soon change, and the life that I live will have a new name.

SCORNED

Do you know the true meaning of a woman scorned? Well it doesn't start when you were born. However, it does begin with the early stages of love that turns sour and it will continue hour after hour. By the time you move on with your life your deepest depression has a sacrifice -- you -- your soul is now scared and your heart is torn in two, what in the hell can you do? Your mind is the strongest thing about you, While your heart is the weakest link get yourself together, think girl, think!!What happened to your mind? You're running out of time, please stop putting your life on the line. For a man who's not worth a dime. When you were a child and punished by your father and mother; you didn't like it so stop letting your man treat you like his little brother. There is someone that will treat you like a queen not a clown and he will never beat you down. A scared soul is something you allow to happen, when the warning signs unfold and your heart is torn; now you have become a woman scorned.

SPIRIT OF THE DAMNED

Moaning, groaning, heavy foot sounds, creaking floors fill our ears. POUND, POUND, POUND. Moving around late at night, spirit of the damned in an out of sight. When your nights are restless and your days drag on you scream "how long must this go on". You're at your wits end it's the agony of defeat, The spirit of the damned walks on two feet. You try not to be mean critize and be tough, spirit of the damned we have had enough. Set in his ways that are gone too far too change. Losing touch with reality is demenshia to blame. Spirit of the damned leave, leave, leave; spirit of the damned we can't breathe. The smell of you feels the air spirit of the damned is everywhere!

MY HEART

The sound of music is love to my heart, feels me with joy right from the start. Music makes memories you hold deep down in your heart. Memories & Music you can't tear them apart, they flow as one and will make you smile real wide. My heart loves memories and my heart loves music, my heart is an open book waiting on a real man to use it.

Thoughts of a woman, a young girl coming of age: It was the summer of 1994, I just turned 23 years old and had 2 kids and in a 5 year relationship that was not what I had hoped it would be. But once again I tried to make the best of it and continue to be the best mother and lady / girlfriend I could be. I know that I am a very head strong person (especially watching my grandmother over the years) but yet I continued to allow the man I choose to be with shed a dark shadow over my life. I was sure he would change and make me the happiest woman on this earth. I truly felt in my heart that he loved me very much but he had no idea or clue on how to show me and/or treat me. However, he did show me that he loved my daughter just as much as he loved his son and that he really wanted to be a part of the family. I just always known that I did not feel special to him in the way a woman wants her man to make her feel wanted. I was longing for that special moment that he would love me with his words, mind & soul not just his body.

CUM AGAIN

I loved the idea, the look on your face and how you watched with grace, it made me cum. That rush, that thrust, that sound as it was going down made me cum. The soft slippery tongues touched my body vigorously as my hands griped my breast continuously made me cum. As our bodies build up heat and juices begin to flow, don't cha know, my kitty pours like rain, oh yes I came. When it's over, the thought of you starts over to begin and oh daddy I will cum again....

INSANE

Crazy life, Crazy times, and Crazy people but it is all one in the same. Life is crazy, times are crazy, people are crazy but no one wants to take the blame. They just run and hide their pride because they are ashamed. But an Insane life, brings on Insane times, and causes Insane people. And this is the gateway to a wild wicked mental ride some people cannot hide. Insanity is a phase that we all go through, it's very hard to tame, but we all pull through looking for a change. That alone can make anyone feel insane.

SHE

I've always wondered how SHE managed to stay in control, even how SHE maintained her household. How could SHE continue to show love and support and keep a smile, knowing hard times were keeping her down. SHE has 2 kids in her home, is there a king that sits on a throne. SHE gives and SHE gives with each breath, SHE gives, and SHE gives till there is nothing left. SHE stands strong and is very swift; SHE has a heart of gold that is her gift.

LOST (SOUL)

Help me, find me, I'm lost in life. The womb I came from is no longer near, my soul has a void, and it sheds a tear. I move aimlessly through this life, I have issues and problems I can't make right. My soul is cold my body is weak, my mind is lost and my heart bleeds. As I stand still and pay attention to my surroundings it becomes oh so clear. My soul is not lost it's always been here. My children are my world the give me reason to be, my soul is not lost, my soul is free.

ROLES WE PLAY

What you set forth to do on any day is simply the role you play in life. Sometimes you are a flop, sometimes you are hit, most of the time you take a dive and that's not right. One day out of the week you attempt to unwind, you want to chill, sit and recline. That's when your new role to play shows its face and unwind turns to rewind...... Is dinner ready? I can't find my phone!.... ARGH!!! give me space, leave me alone. Order calls, night had fall and it's time for the last role we play to appear. But in a blink of an eye the words we cry about the day that's near to begin, the thought of the roles to start again gives us hope that the world we know will continue the roles we play in.

DAD

You meet a lady that's fine; you wine and dine her all the time. While you're having fun you think it's hot and it's not so bad, 9 months later you're a dad. You have created this life from a happy moment, now you look so sad because you had no intentions on being a dad. As this child grows your pockets start to sag, reality sets in damn you're a dad. 16 years later the kid is about grown, making bad decisions and mistakes on his own. With that image on his face it takes you to that place that reminds you of his dad. Yet the grandfather is raising him and that's pretty darn sad. Dad where are you; mommy didn't plan to raise me alone, she loves me like a king who sits on a throne. There's only a few things she can teach me, the rest I have to learn on my own. I came in this world like a thief in the night a thunderous storm an awful fright. Mommy doesn't have much and she is not mad, mommy is my mother she is not my dad.

I remember one Christmas long ago when I was 12 years old. My cousins and I stayed up all night trying to see how many presents we each had underneath the Christmas tree. I find myself smiling a lot when I think of those days, that's when we were young and pure. You never know exactly how your life will change once you cross that line from being a little girl to a full grown woman. It's really a big leap if you don't have anyone to coach you on life, sex & relationships. My life had taken a big plunge into adult hood by the age of 19 I had a daughter and was hot as a fire cracker. By the age of 21 that fire in me was in full flame, I had given birth to a baby boy, I was with his father and we had our own little family. But I continued to party all the time, hung out late to the wee hours of the morning and was not really thinking about work or paying any bills. I told my self-lots of times that I am my own women, no one rules me but me. I love the night life, the music, the atmosphere, and the dancing (something I really love to do). Although for several years my son's father never wanted me to explore my own world or even experience life for what it was worth. I continued to comply with his wishes, however, when I chose to sit and write my poetry (poems) he would make me feel as though I was writing a letter of some sort to another man. He seriously feud and fought with me over my passion, I was mentally & verbally abused by him for wanting to put my thoughts and feelings on paper. I can't even think of any moment where he was interested in my writings nor my love for words. And that's when the physical abuse begins.

THE FEELINGS OF LIFE WITH ALL IT'S UPS AND DOWNS

You come out the womb upside down; your feet are the last thing that touches solid ground. If you enter this world without a sound the doctor gives you're a bottom a slap your mother frowns. As you scream and breathe in life, your parents smile in awh because they know there will be a sacrifice. The home you are taken too becomes your new domain, by the time you begin to crawl you recognize your name. When you take your first steps you wobble and fall, these are signs later written on the wall. The wall of life that catches your dreams it even catches some of the bad things. You start to grow swift and quick, you mother takes care of you if you become sick. As you reach a certain point in age you don't want to be bothered, you start to take on traits just like your father. Now you're all grown and making your own choices, no more listening to us; you ignore our voices. The company you keep reflects an image on you; sometimes the ones you love don't love you. When your heart is broken and you're all alone, reality sets in then you call your mother on the phone. Your father gives you advice; your mother remembers the sacrifice. A few months have passed, the word came fast that they found you face down and hurt real bad. The day was weary the sky was grey your father could not speak and your mother was astray. This was wild, it could not be true, How could this happen what did he do. As your parents mourn the loss of their child they remember the feelings of life with all its up's and down's. Now as they prepare to lay you to rest, their heart has been pounding,,, right through their chest. The feelings of life with all its ups and downs, gives you levels of joy that will make you laugh or frown.

LOVE OR HATE

Ask him if he loves you, ask him if he cares. Is he mesmerized when he looks into your eyes or does his presence make you cry. Does his smile warm you up or creep you out. Will his voice sooth you or fear you, how can he adore you and still tell you lies, does he bore you but you still want to try. Will his hand pound you his words scorn you or his fist gives you a black eye. Ask him, why don't you, your heart needs to know or are you his wife material or some kind of hoe. Ask him what are his plans of being your man, does he intend on sticking around, or does he plan on keeping you down. Ask him before it is too late, ask him......... Is this love or is this hate.

ALL OF YOU

Two eyes, Two hands, Two legs, Two feet, Two souls come together now Two hearts beat. When things come in pairs you tend to fill whole, now life has a new meaning and your world is not so cold. Only our creator knows the master plan of putting pairs together as one to stand. All of you is what I need, All of you is what we need, All of you is All of me, All of you completes me. One nose, One mouth, One private part, One face, brings on One love when we embrace. All of you brings out the best in me, All of you makes my heart sing, All of me is All of you, All of me is into you.

ESCAPE

Close your eyes, think of a special place, and hold your heart with a smile to embrace. Remember that moment when your thoughts were free and clear, Escape to that moment and I will be near. Take a deep breath, give yourself a hug, and laugh out loud with a scream as if you've seen a bug. Escape to that moment I'll be right there to share, peek around the corners of your mind,,,, I'll be at your side, never behind, yes,,,,, right there. Escape with me, to the thoughts in your mind, we'll find each other there, time after time. A mental Escape plan is always a need, This mental Escape plan is just for you and me.

"QUOTE UN-QUOTE"

Who are you? Why are you here? Did you come to bring fear? My life was in a mess long before you spoke, but this is my life, not a silly joke. Who told you that? Why are you making a scene? Did you think I'd run away? I am not afraid I will stand strong. Even when you point out all my wrongs. My life was a complete mess before you considered it a joke, but this is my life no one asked you to spoke; "Quote Un-Quote" If you ask me you are the joke because my life has reason, so go somewhere and choke.

When I was just about 22 years old I had a few part time jobs near home. Because I did not have my own car I had to rely on the mass transportation aka "The Iron Pimp". I was attending Jordan College and on the dean's list every semester, I held 2 jobs inside the school (head librarian & Office night clerk) the hours were not that bad because I had a few breaks between classes which allowed me to work. I have always been able to make lots of friend's quick, so it was not a surprise to me when the entire school knew my name. My son's father soon began to have classes at Jordan College and played on the college basketball team. This was truly a life learning lesson for me; seriously he also was very popular with meeting new people including lots of new female classmates. I can admit I was a bit jealous at first but one lady in particular stood out; This lady not only wanted to be his friend but mine as well.

DIRT

When soil is dry, it becomes hard and crumbly. Just like a sweet soul, that's sad and lonely. You know a little water showers the ground with love, just like a smile can cuddle your heart with the sun's rays; it just gives you a good start for better days. When your down and you feel low as dirt, think about that moist soil first. It has been drizzled with water to make it feel at its best. Just like love episodes can put your mind to the test. If you let your heart go and be kicked all around, you'll find your spirits slithering on the ground. Exert your mind to be free and unhurt then there will be no need to waddle around in dirt.

$2

If I had $2 I'd share with you, When you have $2 you hang with your crew. 2 plus 2 equals 4, we could have so much more. If we put our ends together we could manage to take care of each other better. The novelty of spreading the wealth tends to bypass me; I am the broken side of epitome. Down to my last $2 a women like me will make it stretch, although a man like you will place his last $2 on a bet.

TRY ME ON FOR SIZE

I know i am short; something like 5 ft 2, but my heart is big and sure to mesmerize you. I may be somewhat thick around the waist, but this sister does have taste. My face is round my nose is pudgy, but the love I bring is oh so lovely. Supersize me and I'll Mega size you, my only wish is to cater to you. Yes I am light brown, with stretch marks and scars; I know my looks are nothing like the high paid stars. I weigh about 158, I work out a little and I feel great. I may not be that main piece or prize, but you will never know if you don't try me on for size.

GIVE AND TAKE

Give me a moment I hear you, Why should I listen I'm through with you. Take a moment to hear yourself, Do you understand, you are not husband material you're just a simple man. You give what you want and always take what you need, no matter if the results make me bleed. Give me some space, yes I need to replace you. Why do I need to keep enduring the bad guy in you. Take a second to hear my cry I certainly wish you were another guy. I'll take my strength back and give you the boot, this give and take lesson has shown me the true you.

SAY SOMETHING

When I speak an echo fills the room. I see four corners and sold walls but no windows to see through. The air is light my hands are balled tight, because my mind is putting up such a fight. I'm trying to communicate I want to speak aloud; I want to be heard not punished like a child. Say something, why don't you. Let me know where I stand I'm lost inside my own head, a wicked game plan. Say Something if you're on the outside looking in, Say something please, especially if you're my friend. Say Something loudly because I can't hear at all, this room I am stuck in has no doors nor halls.

EASY DOES IT

You overcome adversity all while learning something new, has to be the best thing that could ever happen to you. Passing every class making a good grade, brings out a better quality of life lessons gained. Stand up for your words and hold on to the moment of truth, these happy times make you want to share a smile with a neighbor or two. Whistle as you walk and skip with the beat; give yourself a high five because every day is a living treat.

OUTTER THOUGHTS

You see me, I see you..... what oh what can we do? If people see you as I look into your soul, people will see me with a frown on my face as I get old. Where is the joy my heart needs to sing, it seems to you my life doesn't mean a thing.

SOME DAYS

Some days are better than others, yet we start them out the same. Some days are filled with joy, Some days we just complain. Don't continue to let repetition lead your brain open up your thoughts let life do it's thing; unless it is certain that you are insane.

By the time I was 25 (as my kids said half way to 50) my life begun to have some sort of meaning. I truly felt like a woman, who had been drug through mud yet my mind was clean and free of any negativity that I had witnessed earlier in life. I began to speak publicly about my hardships and setbacks. Although a little bit of embracement filled my soul, I knew it was best to get certain things off my chest and off my heart. My baby daddy did not agree to me saying things about our relationship to others. It was difficult for me to make him understand that speaking about my problems; our problems were healthy for me, better yet healthy for us. I learned from my mom that no one can tell your story better than you and my dad would make sure that I knew the meaning of any and every word that spewed out of my mouth. Of course he dubbed me over as motor mouth, which was a funny family joke about me as a child. I still had thoughts of having a loving husband, a lovely home, a decent vehicle and a few dollars to fold. But once again, of course reality has to show up and show out.

THE 3 BROTHERS

I only knew 2 my dad said it was 3; he showed us pictures and an explanation on how this could be. Years had gone by and still I only grew up with 2 my dad let us know that Lil Pete was in prison for a few. As destiny unfolds the days come and go, I found myself visiting a prison with my cousin to see her friend, and how could I know. That this dude who looked like my dad bent the corner with his pinky finger in the air, and my mind started buzzing. Hey I remembered this guy from high school who always hollered "give me a dollar" as he chuckled walking down the halls. On the inside I laughed the outside I cried, as I told Andre and Jock the story my dad could no longer hide. This is my brother, as he approached and took a seat, my brother from another mother my dad called him lil Pete.

THE 3 SISTERS

I am glad that I'm my mom's only girl, however, when I was told I have 2 sisters that changed my world. I could not wait to meet them; I needed to know their names. My dad smiled while my mom tried to explain. Peaches has always been around, while blue eyes came and went. I never really understood that part, those words I really didn't get. Upon my dad's last days on this earth he spoke of one other little girl that his seed helped to birth. My inner thoughts were extremely happy, I have 3 sisters and we share the same pappy. As we all have endured on another, I can safely say I wouldn't change a thing, this is as right as it can be. This life has given me 3 sisters who I love unconditionally.

ENTERTAIN ME

I live to laugh and love all the while you cry and scream to hate all that I am.

CASH. RULES. EVERYTHING. AROUND. ME

Closed mouth speaks of C.R.E.A.M, Open eyes leads to sights unseen. Closed hearts burn to the core; these are things we all adore. When you think you deserve much more than you have, C.R.E.A.M smacks your face real hard and fast. A sensitive ear hears so loud sometimes a fist or an open hand can bring you down. C.R.E.A.M can make you proud or bring you to your knees while life laughs at you like a clown. C.R.E.A.M is the outcome of life on the edge, C.R.E.A.M the only way to make your bread.

EMBRACE YOUR SELF

We tend to embrace the opposite of what we seek, do you really understand the power beneath. The wicked soul of others, the crazy images in their mind, the awful thoughts they keep deep down inside. The world we know is full of mayhem and deceit, you have to be careful, be strong and stand on your own two feet. Live your life as you know best, never let the world put you to the test. When you live you score when you love there is so much more. Be the love you carry with in, it will give your heart time to mend. Intercept the moment in time that life and love tend to rewind. Embrace yourself sit and sip some wine, then you will see that all of our precious moments will be reveled in time.

You know how life gives you subliminal messages from time to time. Well I can't help but to recall the images in my mind that one life time ago, I was somehow involved with President Lincoln. I remember going to huckleberry railroad with the seventh grade class of Whittier High School and visiting the small cabins on site. Each cabin was filled with furniture from the 1800's and antique artifacts that for some reason I remembered. As I entered the log cabin home (replica) for President Abraham Lincoln, my body began to shiver and shake because the images in my mind were so vivid; That I was able to say which room we were about to enter and explain how each item in the room was used. I think I was a house servant for him, seriously I had thoughts and feelings that I could not explain to myself how come I was able to embrace those moments from that era since I was born on April 19, 1971 exactly 106 years and 4 days from his death. Ironically enough my son was born on February 13, 1991 which happens to be 182 years and 1 day from Lincoln's birth date, somehow I feel that I am caught in between worlds and the Deja vu phenomenon fills my soul and the events are so real to me that I am so sure I have been here before. That was not the first time I had those visions or feelings about Abraham Lincoln. One time I was watching a movie and it was based on him during the emancipation of slavery, when that Deja vu feeling came again. I cried on so many scenes that you would've thought I was at a family member's funeral. At some point in time I became obsessed with that thought of being on this earth before that I began to research events from those times. Honestly, I believe my mental strength comes from those moments lost in time that I feel so connected too.

YES

No I will not be a follower, because I am a leader. No I cannot be who you want me to be, simply because I stand on my own two feet. No I don't live for you I live for me, just because you try to be who you are not, does not fool me. No my world does not revolve around you, basically because my world equals me. No I cannot, I will not, give you my all just because you say you'll catch me when I fall. No I don't need you to pick me up when the chips are down. Yes my life is complete that's why I wear a smile not a frown, this is why I say YES I am in charge and I wear my own crown.

WILD DAYS & COLD NIGHTS

The sun has gone down, the wind is calm, the air is dry, and you have sweaty palms. The sky is beautiful and the stars are bright, the evening has set upon us as we now we enter the night. Look at the trees, their image is without movement because there is no breeze. It's hard to tell the grass from the dirt as they all blend with the night, a chill has come over your body and yet you have no one to hold you tight. The daylight will soon show its face sure as the misty dew shimmers all over the place. The warmth of the sun covers your body with the start of a new day. It gives you the feeling of being blessed and the hopes that this day you meet your king or queen and feel a little less stressed.

DINNER FOR TWO

A small sip of your smile, a large drink from your life, a nice bite of your heart fulfills my appetite. I plan to taste every inch of you, if I could swallow you whole that's what I would do. This is a sexy dinner a dinner for two. My body is the main dish, my heart is your snack, my breast compliments this meal while my booty is ready for you to smack. My hair is long and strong as you feed from the back, please hold on, no need to lack. This dinner for two is hot and ready, everything around us moves while this moment is steady. As we place this order to eat, drink, slip and slide, our reservations feast on love making and now it's time. Eat me up gobble me down; let me taste the nectar that comes out of your crown. When you moan my name, my plate over flows, as the heat generates moisture your lips gently blow. All over me and then I'm all over you I enjoyed this sexy dinner, this dinner for two.

TREE

When you see trees stand side by side no tree is exactly the same. But when you pull a tree out of the ground, it looks the same even upside down. It gives you belief that this could be true, humans and trees have deep roots. Human's birth lives while trees birth leaves, it's all a part of Gods creations just like the birds and the bees. You cannot see the forest without the trees and you cannot hear Gods voice unless you are on bended knees. He has a message that's loud and clear as long as you see trees he is here have no fear. The moment man destroys one another and all the trees on this land it off sets the masters plan. So plant a tree give life, remember he gave his only son as a sacrifice. A tree gives an image we need to see: Have deep roots, stand up, stand strong, be who you were created to be and you won't go wrong.

HOW I FEEL

People always say I know how you feel, or I feel you. But truth be told no one knows, it's all about the story you tell and how it unfolds. The image you project and the words you speak gives a person reason to think. How I feel is even a mystery to me, a thousand and one things run through my mind and I am always running short of time. When you are asked, How are you or How have you been or maybe How has life been treating you dear friend. Let's you know someone has been thinking of you or maybe wondering how you have managed in life. How I feel is written on my face, the smile I wear, my loving touch and my warm embrace.

THE COST OF LOVE

At what depth will you go to at the cost of love, is there a method to the madness? Does the heart ever learn? How many times will it love before it crash and burns? The level of love cannot be measured like a liquid in a measuring jar; the heart has no bottom I've learned thus far. At what level in life will you know that your soul is complete? Have you met that certain one that makes your heart skip a beat? The heart has its own powers it can be soft or cold it can even be solid as a brick tower. Is there a price to pay when it comes to the heart, Can you actually own emotions of the heart as if you are in control. Does the cost of love come with a guarantee, which will show the special effects of true love meant to be. The cost of love can take you by surprise, the cost of love has many different disguise, the cost of love can make or break you even if the cost of love consumes and takes you.

1998 I was 27 years old, my children were growing fast and my relationship was fastly spiraling out of control. It seemed the older I got the more I thought about where my life would be when I turned 30 years old. Did I really want to marry a man who could not financially support me, or even support me with the dreams I had of becoming a writer. I asked my self-lots of questions when it came to life and love. Sometimes the answers I came up with did not always fit the situation. I did however; give that man the benefit of the doubt with certain demands. If he wanted to continue to be in my life he needed to get and maintain a job to help support the family and also learn to love me more with affection and trust. I never thought that I would spend the rest of my life with anyone but him. But as you and I both know time has a way of showing you the truth. There were times when I was ready to walk out on him and just raise my kids on my own. But the grown women in me wanted to have a man in my life so that my kids would know that good family values began from a home filled with a mother & a father. But it was so many things that gave me vibes of doubt that I was beginning to get scared of becoming someone's wife. Especially his wife, the man whom makes me feel bad about myself sometimes. The man that keeps me crying more than keeping a smile on my face. But how could I not think of the days when I felt his love and when we conceived my son. I cannot deny that we had lots of good times but way too many bad times was all I could see.

SLEEPLESS

I went to sleep alone on one cold night, everything around me was dark, and I grabbed my pillow tight. As I drifted off to sleep I had visions of you, my body felt warm (oh how I adore you)... The bed began to hold me with a grip that I like, kind of reminds me of you in my dreams at night. The warmth of the cover touched me in such a way, that my mind began to wonder of you in that kind of way. Soon as the suns light, was bright, a smile came upon my face. I opened my eyes, the image of you was still in sight, I had a dream, a dream that lasted all night.

MY NAME

I've been told that I am as beautiful as my name. When I smile you smile yet you can't see my pain. Even when my tears flow like rain one would never know all that my life contains. I'm full of love, so grateful for life, my mind is filled with joy, and my soul pays a price. I stand tall with my short frame, I would give you my all...just call my name. When hard times show up, my instincts show out, the shoes I walk in are so wore out. There are 9 letters in my name, each letter has its on way to twist, twirl and tame. Each letter is so magnificent they are all individual statements of my name.

T is for thoughtful
E is for epic
R is for real
R is for ready
A is for always
L is for loves deep within
I is for important
S is for satisfying
A is for alluring

EYES

Look into someone's eyes; it's a way to see inside the soul. It will show you much more than what's told. Some eyes are small and cold some eyes are big and bold, the eyes say more than your mouth can withhold. I see what you feel when I look into your eyes, your eyes tell a story your soul try's to hide. Be cautious and beware the looks you give someone you may share more than you care. The eyes are the gateway that opens up the center of you, shows the world what is embedded deep within the inside thoughts of you. So don't try to lie or cover up the truth, the look in your eye will give proof. Your eyes give a message so make no mistake, looking at someone may be as tragic as jumping in a lake.

SHARING

I'll give you some of me if you give me some of you. Please don't take me for a fool and I won't play you close. You give me lots of great feelings; I'll give you my heart. Make me a believer of all you know to be true, and my dear I will be all into you. My world is an open book read me fast or read me slow I'll be your lover I am not your hoe. You are a test I would like to pass; I'll make the grade because I'm a lady with class. Show me how you live day to day and I'll share my deepest thoughts with you and never lead you astray.

BODY MOVEMENT

Watching you walk is such a treat; I love how you move with ease it makes my heart skip a beat. I feel a tingling sensation when your near, my body screams out come get it, I'm right here. When I approach you my legs feel weak, my arms like jelly then I can't speak. Looking at your massive size makes me feel like a child winning a prize. The thought of you with all that swag gives me a feeling I've never had. When your lips move as you talk, my lips move as I walk, closer and closer to feel your touch my body tremors oh so much. My small frame is ready to be tamed and release the beast that lies deep within; your body movement makes me want to be more than just your friend.

It was the winter of 1999, I continued to work on the relationship with my son's father and he began to show improvement. He started a new job; he was more loving and trying to be supportive to me when it came to the home and our relationship. That's when he asked me for the third time to marry him, I was feeling loved and so I said yes. At one point I started to second guess my answer because from time to time his ugly ways would surface. I watched him closely then, I even watched how he treated other people and how his reactions were to some of the things that a husband or family man should do. I must say I had my doubts. But once again he put on a good show for others but behind closed doors he was that same man that made me feel bad. The gears were already turning and the wedding date was near, I had cold feet but because I am a woman of my word I continued to proceed with the marriage. My daughter was about 12 years old and she was really not buying the ideal of me getting married to a man who was not her father. She made it very clear that it would be odd because she would be the only one with a different last name. That alone gave me more doubts of getting married, but I stuck with the original plan. Deep down inside I really did not want to make this major change in my life because I was very uncertain of how far it would go and or how long it would be before his old ways or shall I say his true inner self showed back up. I was caught between a rock and a hard place, my heart was weak and my mind was heavy. I began to realize the truth, and that was so scary that I almost called off the wedding. But you should know a little bit about me now, I stand strong throughout any adversity. Just like all my other endeavors, this too shall pass. So we got married February 18th 2000 in Ohio at the local court house. Then we had a reception April 26th 2000 at the local 598 in flint.

SARCASTIC

My mind is clear, my thoughts are too, and my vision to succeed in this world will come true. All my life I have planned to be on top, even when all my plans tend to flop. I will never give up, I will never give in. Even if the struggle is more than I can bare, I'll just pick up a pen; express how I feel, but you may not want me to share. Things in my life don't revolve around you, my life is hard but I manage to pull through. Some things I say may offend you, I am sorry if that is true. However, what I say comes from the heart thoughts deep within that lay dormant in the dark. My life is no fairy tale this is true, things I do should not matter to you.

THIS IS IT

You find yourself looking for a way out, that right moment to leave. When the walls are closing in it feels like you can't breathe, you think this is it; that right moment to leave. Each day seems to never bring you joy and each night you feel as if your life has a void. This is it; that right moment to leave so you gather your thoughts and proceed to move on time to plant new seeds. Every moment you calculate the drastic moments for steps to take for that right moment to leave; you say this is it.

HOLD ON

Some things and some people never change it's like living life on repeat the same ole song over and over again... Hold on, doing the same thing over and over reminds me of a never ending story.... Hold on, I promise this time it will be different begins to sound like a set up or a demand.... Hold on, you are a father, a son, a man.... Hold on, stop holding me back, Hold on, start taking up the slack and quit putting my life on pause...

ENERGY

I feel you as you enter the room, like a sunny day when the flowers bloom. The scent of you excites me and that's such a thrill. My mind is set on pleasing you, I'm so for real. The Energy you carry has a magnetic pull; it gives you wings just like red bull. When you speak the ground beneath you shakes, make no mistakes I'm yours to take. I feel your energy flow over my body and cover me like baby oil, your energy makes me feel good and your energy got me spoiled.

UNTITLED

Word to the wise: Believe in yourself. Never expect to be encouraged by those who calculate you're every move. They are an understatement, full of bad vibes to weaken your strength and the ground you walk on.

#REALTALK

There comes a time when you just have to look at yourself for who and what you are. No one can justify the inner true you. However, when you force or falsify your existence into any situation. You give a certain aura that tends to lead people astray. Once your ugly outer image leaks out, it leaves a foul smell in the air.

As I reflect back on different levels of my life, it makes me wonder. Did I do things in a respectable manor, did I follow the right steps to become a woman, or do I have what it takes to survive in this wicked world. My grandmother usually comes to mind when I start to thinking like that. I know that we all live our lives the way we want, but when you have children (in my case two) that depend on you and look up to you there is no time to second guess or fold. I also think of the times when I was much younger and my mother was still with us (oh how I miss her). We all take for granted how pure our hearts were as a child and that the adult in your life was supreme. I have always loved and respected the fact that my elders were the ones in charge and that they had the power to control my universe. Now that I am a mother and wife I had to make some more adjustments in my life that I do not believe I was really truly ready for. I have always heard that life will throw you a curve ball in the blink of an eye. It's funny how different things you are around and are accustomed to begin to tell the story of the real you. When I was about 7yrs old my granddad used to watch a lot of westerns and rodeo shows. I never knew why I just knew he had a cowboy kind of attitude and he loved his Rifle(s). Johnny Gist, aka Buddy, better known as Shotgun. He was not one for games, when it came to family. He was a hardworking man but he also was a heavy drinking man too. I could never understand why my grandmother hardly ever spoke to him let alone sleep with him. The family knew my granddad loved her and she loved him, they just had a distant relationship. It is hard to believe that two people in a marriage could have so much anger built up that it forms a brick wall between them. I watched them live this way until I was 18 (that's when my grandfather passed away). My grandmother Minne Gist, never remarried nor did she entertain the presence of another man. However, that lonely look in her eyes and the sadness on her face shows that she has never been happy. The pain in her heart derives from being an unhappy wife for so long. I also believe that she has never forgave herself for sticking with a man that never made her happy nor made her feel special. As much as I love my gram (nickname the grandkids call her), I will not live that way and be unhappy till one of us goes home to meet our creator.

FADE

My vision was strong when I thought of you, my heart was warm it made my smile so wide, I loved you way deep down inside. The feelings you gave me, the world could not touch, my life with you meant so much. Now my vision is fuzzy and not so clear, when you speak to me I can't hear. Your cold ways has lead me to lonely days, I never thought life with you would be this way. My thoughts of love are gone when I think of you, all I see is the wrongs you never made right. It's time to give up this never ending fight, I think of you less as I fade into a new life.

GREY MOMENT

If you are doing it right I got that appetite to endure it all kinds of ways, I am always hungry for you no matter what we do, I can take it, I am a big girl I will be brave.

You slayed me with passion behind closed doors, my mind and body wants you so much more. I'm your submissive I enjoy being your sex slave, just like the book 50 shades of grey. There is a dark moment, for brighter days that shade in between is a misty grey, my mind holds a lot of secrets my body will follow, give me your best shot I just may swallow. My intentions to ride this moment like a wicked storm is all the reason my body swarms. I'll give you a special part of my heart; I hope you will do the same. No need to tame me I am yours to crave, I'll be that platter, your side dish with all the things you like, I'm your lover not your wife.

MY TRUE STATEMENT #1

Things that life throws your way tend to change a few steps you make in life it depends on you, yourself to control the environment you dwell in and the path you are bond to take. When you allow certain issue of life cast a shadow over you it's hard to see the light. Sometimes the tunnel vision of our hearts leads us on a high speed chase.

MY TRUE STATEMENT #2

Just because you think you got it all together, does not mean that anyone else believes in your journey. Sometimes it is better to move forward with great force without making waves. At that point you will finally finish the chapter of a story that seemed to never end.

LIFE LESSONS I'VE LEARNED #1

I cannot help but to wonder why some people look down on others when they are two steps ahead with disgust all the while knowing they were in that same spot two seconds ago.....

LIFE LESSONS I'VE LEARNED #2

When everything you do crumbles, and you feel like there is no hope. Remember that the person next to you (significant other, husband, wife, family, or friend) just might be the reason you are still afloat. People tend to forget who has there back and will catch them when they fall. Even if it means they fall with you. So I ask "Is it that hard to be loyal, gentle, and kind"? Take heed because that support can lose grip and build a bridge with another who equally carries the weight, #realtalk.

As life continues to take me down different avenues, I tend to keep in mind that you only live once. I recall all the holidays and special events that all our loved ones who have passed on have missed. One thing about death is that, it is CERTAIN to happen; the time or day will never be known. As my children are getting older, I am getting much wiser and stronger mentally and physically. I am not afraid to say what I feel and do what I say, I will do. I know that me being head strong or hard headed as some would say makes me appear to be mean or selfish; neither are true by the way. But I am an ARIES the first sign of the zodiac also known as or considered the head. Being married had its moments and some of those moments made me really open my eyes about a lot of issues based on the heart. At one point after our 4th year of marriage (summer of 2004) I had begun to find myself thinking about divorce. We were having problems and I was feeling like he truly did not love me or want to be with me. How could he, when all he did was make me cry. I was so in love with him that I started to overlook all the horrible things he did to me and I would make excuses so that others did not look at him in a bad way (although I kept the side eye on him) I always made sure he knew as well as everyone else that my love for him was strong. As the years went by that blind screen I was holding up was actually the brick wall starting to take form between us. Some days it would be torn down by good deeds and loving acts. Then some days it felt like 3 to 4 layers was added per day. 15 years of my life with a man that did not complete me was starting to get old and cold. I still loved and cared for him and I have always tried to give him chance after chance after chance to make me happy and show me (and tell me) the love he proclaims he has for me was real. There is no way I want to grow old unhappy and unloved. I have seen lots of people go through life as an unhappy couple and live together as if it was a daily job with a routine.

THE DIFFERENCE BETWEEN SCHOOL AND LIFE

In school, you are taught a lesson and then given a test. In life, you are given a test that teaches you a lesson.

A THOUGHT

If I could mend the world with one thought I would, if I could change a person's cold heart I would. If living life means anything at all to us as a generation we as a people should learn that humans make mistakes. The key is to learn from them not dwell in them. So open your eyes, close your mouth, think with your heart, feel with your mind understand me and take your time.

THE ROCK

So rough around the edges, yet smooth to the touch, your mass is huge and a bit too much. You are a rock that's settled into the ground, you are the rock I can hardly move around. I tried to hold you and uplift your dead weight, but you never budged my heart was too heavy and ready to break, to be unplugged. The world is filled with many different rocks for one to pick and choose, some big, some small, some you collect and some you lose. Most rocks withstand the test of time, some just crumble to pieces and form a dusty line. The rock that lies in my path tends to block my way, it is bold, it is cold, it never moves it just sits and stays.

redbonetrouble His SMILE stole the spotlight her EXPRESSION stole the moment #move lmao

MY DEDICATION

When considering all the valuable things life has to offer you. I am very happy to say that my life's greatest gifts were given to me by my only daughter (Jeree), my first born child. Ja'Nyah and Jabari, you two have empowered my life more than anything I could imagine. I can only hope that my words of life, love, peace, wisdom, and happiness brings an understanding into your hearts about me. As life continues to lead me into my own future, I am not certain if I will be here long enough to see you two live life and find love. Our creator only knows that time or that moment. Until then, I will continue to grow, write and enjoy life for what it's worth. This is my dedication to the both of you with high hopes that you remember me always. That you remember the love I have for you because I most certainly feel the love you have for me. I also hope that you learn from me in the years to come. The love I hold in my heart for you both is past unconditional and forever. May you always know and understand GiGi loves you. And it is because of you both that I promise to live life to the fullest with all its ups and downs..

Dedicated to:
Ja'Nyah Renae Brown
Jabari Romonce Brown Jr.

The passage below was written by my daughter when she was in 7th grade. It touched me so that I've held on to it since then. I would like to share it with you all I truley believe that my inspirations starts with my children and her words at such a young age reminded me of all my trials and tribulations. Enjoy:

I WANT TO SEE MY GRANDBABY WALK:

I was born in August of 1987. I had a young mother and a very ill grandmother. I don't remember her, but everyone says I act like her. I've always thought, "How can I act like someone I don't even know? A complete stranger". When I relly think about it, it makes sense. I don't act like my mom, I have my dad's attitude, and my personality is like how everyone describes my grandmother. A fun, loving person, and always willing to help someone in need. My grandmother knew that she would pass soon and her last wish was to see me take my first steps.

In December of 1987, my grandmother was not getting any better. She started to become very weak, but that didn't stop her from being around me. For Christmas, she got me a snow white polar bear with the numbers "1987" knitted on the bear's hat. Everyone said that I used to carry it everywhere I went. To stores, and even the bathroom. They said that the bear and I were inseparable, and that the bear was my shadow.

In April of 1988, close to the end of the month, I took my 1st steps. I was only 8 1/2 months old. It's very unusual and rare to see an 8 1/2 month old baby walking, but I think God did that because he knew my grandmother was about to pass away soon. On May 1, 1988 my grandmother passed away. She left behind a daughter, two sons, a mother, three sisters, and four brothers. The most important thing that she didn't leave behind was memories of a granddaughter who made her wish come true. Till this day, I still have the snow white bear whom I named "Mr. Gene White". I named him after my grandmother's middle name, Jean, and the color of his fur, white. She died a happy woman and she is truly missed by all.

Rest in Heaven Linda Jean Gist

Printed in the United States
By Bookmasters